BEGINNING SOLO Guitar

The Beatles

T0085621

ISBN 978-1-4768-7719-8

HAL•LEONARD® CORPORATION

7777 W. BLUEMOUND RD. P.O. BOX 13819 MILWAUKEE, WI 53213

Visit Hal Leonard Online at
www.halleonard.com

GUITAR NOTATION LEGEND

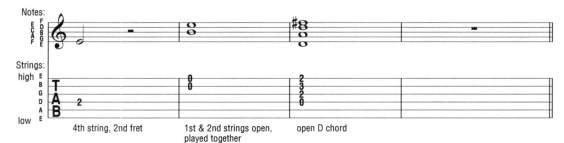

THE MUSICAL STAFF shows pitches and rhythms and is divided by bar lines into measures. Pitches are named after the first seven letters of the alphabet.

TABLATURE graphically represents the guitar fingerboard. Each horizontal line represents a string, and each number represents a fret.

4th string, 2nd fret   1st & 2nd strings open, played together   open D chord

HALF-STEP BEND: Strike the note and bend up 1/2 step.

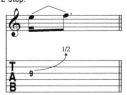

WHOLE-STEP BEND: Strike the note and bend up one step.

GRACE NOTE BEND: Strike the note and immediately bend up as indicated.

SLIGHT (MICROTONE) BEND: Strike the note and bend up 1/4 step.

BEND AND RELEASE: Strike the note and bend up as indicated, then release back to the original note. Only the first note is struck.

PRE-BEND: Bend the note as indicated, then strike it.

VIBRATO: The string is vibrated by rapidly bending and releasing the note with the fretting hand.

PALM MUTING: The note is partially muted by the pick hand lightly touching the string(s) just before the bridge.

HAMMER-ON: Strike the first (lower) note with one finger, then sound the higher note (on the same string) with another finger by fretting it without picking.

PULL-OFF: Place both fingers on the notes to be sounded. Strike the first note and without picking, pull the finger off to sound the second (lower) note.

LEGATO SLIDE: Strike the first note and then slide the same fret-hand finger up or down to the second note. The second note is not struck.

SHIFT SLIDE: Same as legato slide, except the second note is struck.

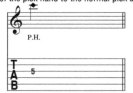

TRILL: Very rapidly alternate between the notes indicated by continuously hammering on and pulling off.

TAPPING: Hammer ("tap") the fret indicated with the pick-hand index or middle finger and pull off to the note fretted by the fret hand.

NATURAL HARMONIC: Strike the note while the fret-hand lightly touches the string directly over the fret indicated.

PINCH HARMONIC: The note is fretted normally and a harmonic is produced by adding the edge of the thumb or the tip of the index finger of the pick hand to the normal pick attack.

TREMOLO PICKING: The note is picked as rapidly and continuously as possible.

VIBRATO BAR DIVE AND RETURN: The pitch of the note or chord is dropped a specified number of steps (in rhythm), then returned to the original pitch.

VIBRATO BAR SCOOP: Depress the bar just before striking the note, then quickly release the bar.

VIBRATO BAR DIP: Strike the note and then immediately drop a specified number of steps, then release back to the original pitch.

Additional Musical Definitions

   (accent)   • Accentuate note (play it louder).

   (staccato)   • Play the note short.

D.S. al Coda   • Go back to the sign (𝄋), then play until the measure marked *"To Coda,"* then skip to the section labelled *"Coda."*

D.C. al Fine   • Go back to the beginning of the song and play until the measure marked *"Fine"* (end).

Fill   • Label used to identify a brief melodic figure which is to be inserted into the arrangement.

N.C.   • Harmony is implied.

   • Repeat measures between signs.

• When a repeated section has different endings, play the first ending only the first time and the second ending only the second time.

All My Loving

Words and Music by John Lennon and Paul McCartney

Eight Days a Week

Words and Music by John Lennon and Paul McCartney

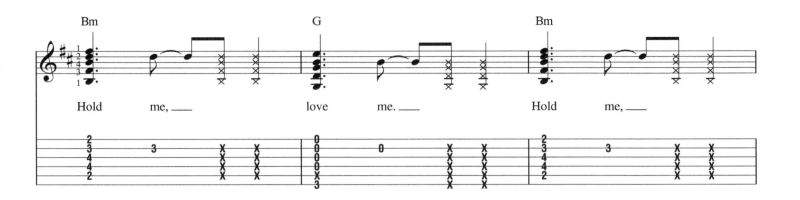

Hold me, ___ love me. ___ Hold me, ___

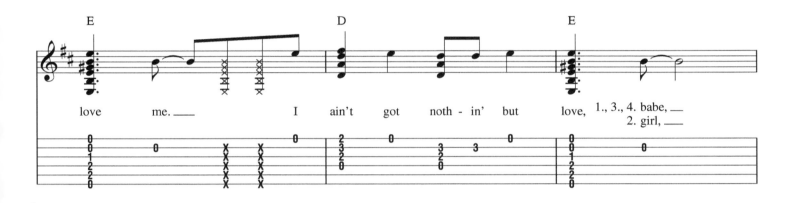

love me. ___ I ain't got noth-in' but love, 1., 3., 4. babe, ___ 2. girl, ___

4th time, To Coda ⊕

Bridge

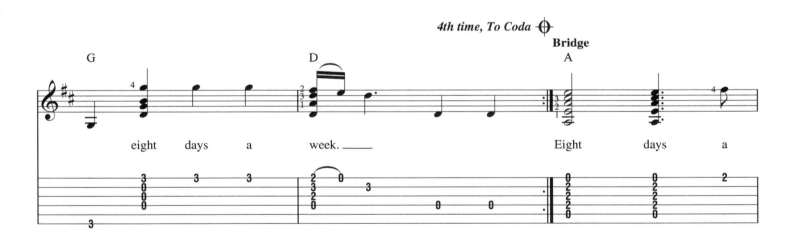

eight days a week. ___ Eight days a

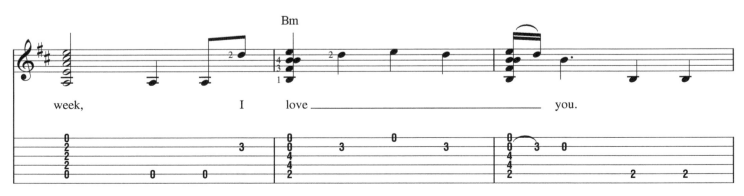

week, I love _____ you.

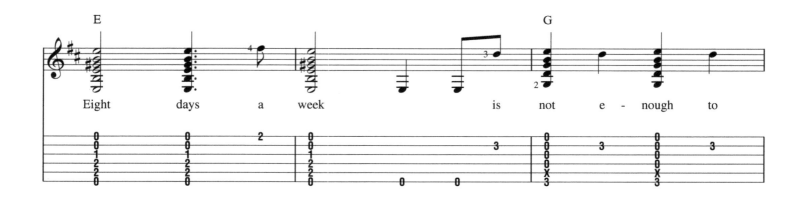

Eight days a week is not e-nough to

1st time, D.S. (no repeat)
2nd time, D.S. al Coda

⊕ **Coda**

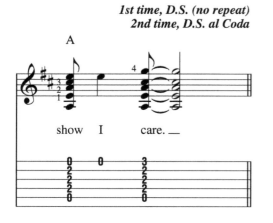

show I care. ___

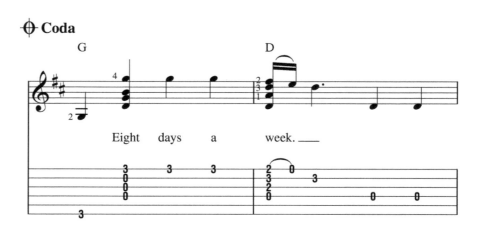

Eight days a week. ___

Outro

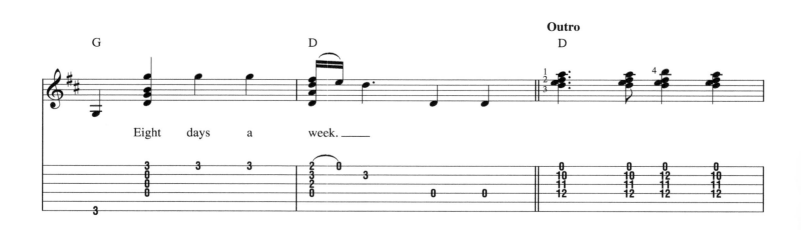

Eight days a week. ___

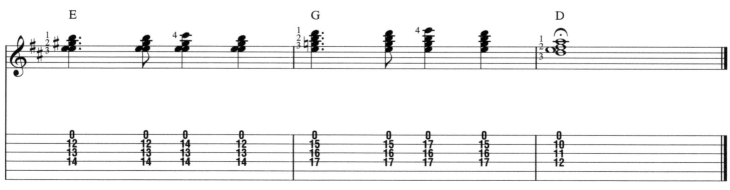

Girl

Words and Music by John Lennon and Paul McCartney

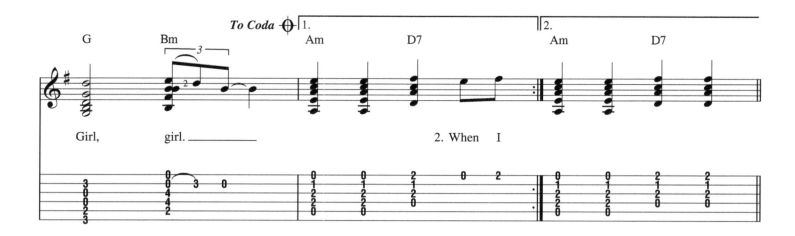

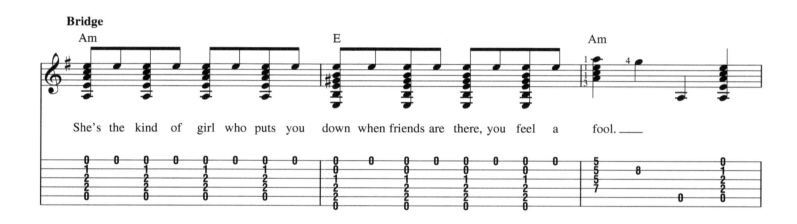

Bridge

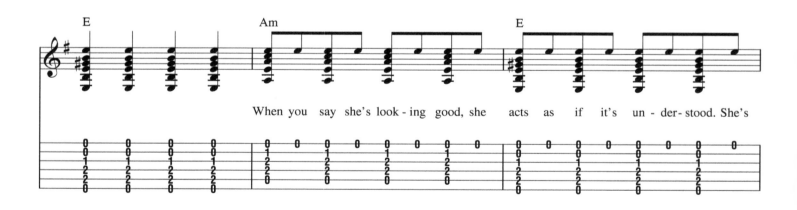

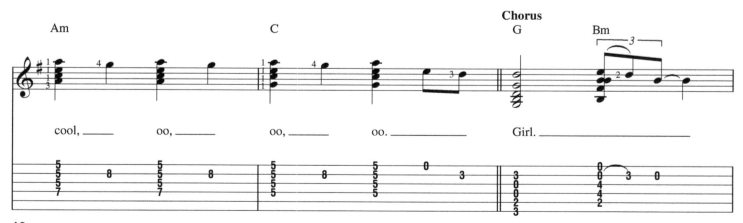

Girl, girl. ___ 3. Was she

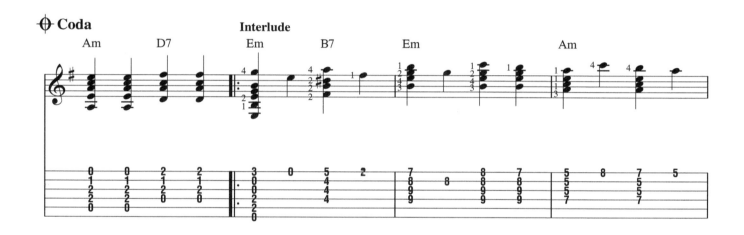

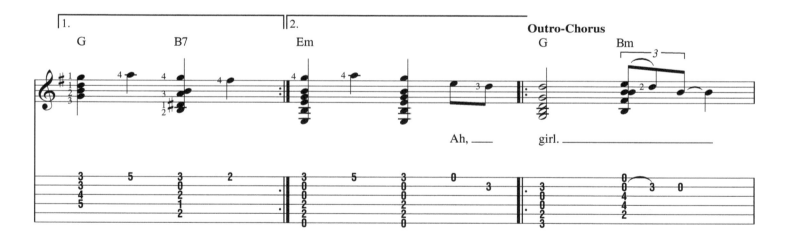

Ah, ___ girl. ___

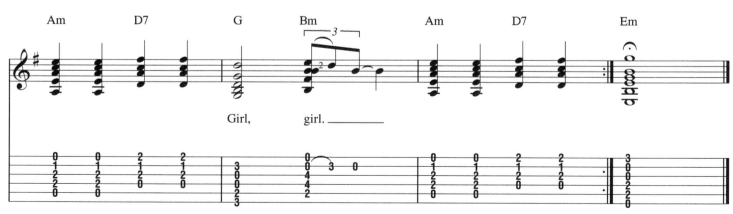

Girl, girl. ___

11

Eleanor Rigby

Words and Music by John Lennon and Paul McCartney

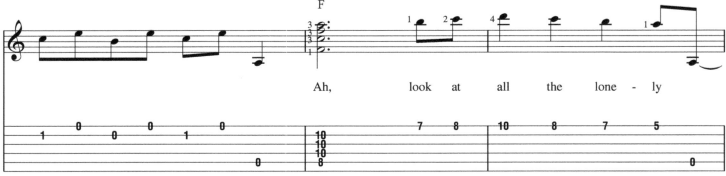

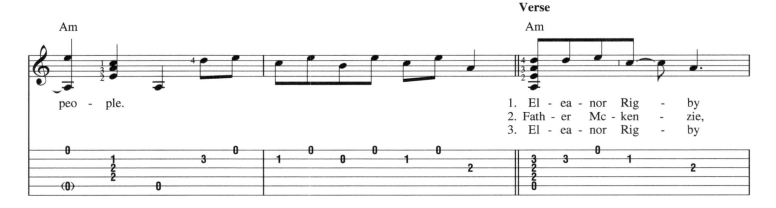

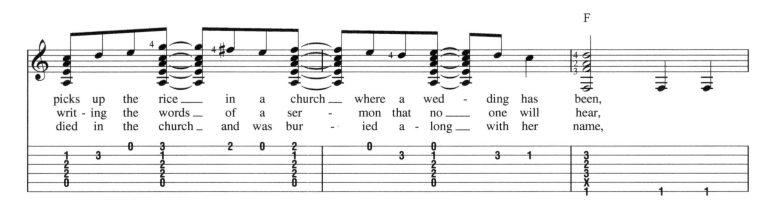

Here Comes the Sun

Words and Music by George Harrison

Bridge

⊕ Coda

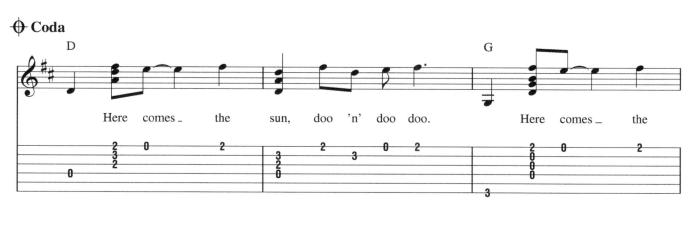

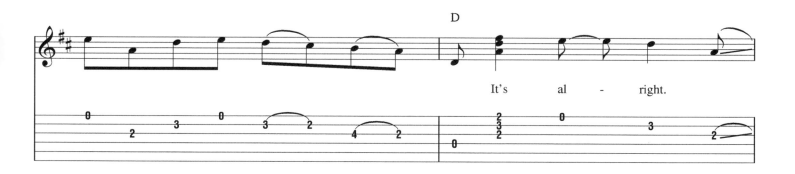

Here, There and Everywhere

Words and Music by John Lennon and Paul McCartney

Hey Jude

Words and Music by John Lennon and Paul McCartney

world up - on ___ your shoul - ders.
some - one to ___ per - form ___ with.

For well you know that it's a
And don't you know that it's just

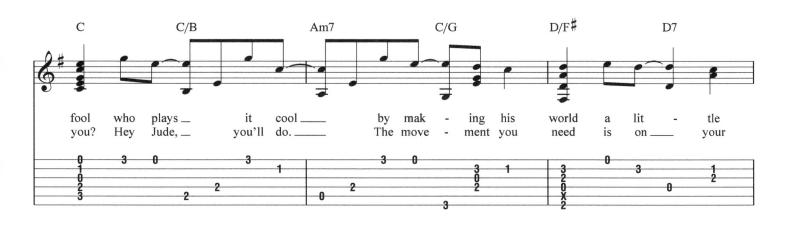

fool who plays ___ it cool ___ by mak - ing his world a lit - tle
you? Hey Jude, ___ you'll do. ___ The move - ment you need is on ___ your

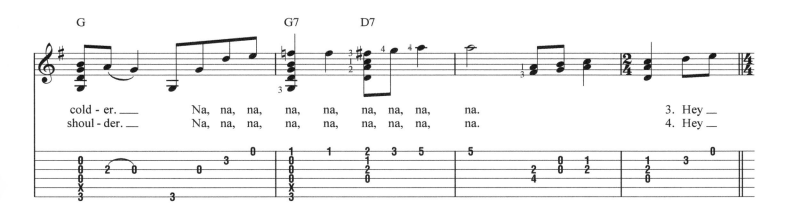

cold - er. ___ Na, na, na, na, na, na, na, na, na.
shoul - der. ___ Na, na, na, na, na, na, na, na, na.

3. Hey ___
4. Hey ___

Verse

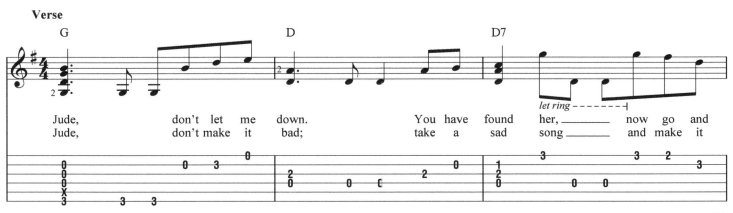

Jude, don't let me down. You have found her, ___ now go and
Jude, don't make it bad; take a sad song ___ and make it

let ring - - - - - - - -

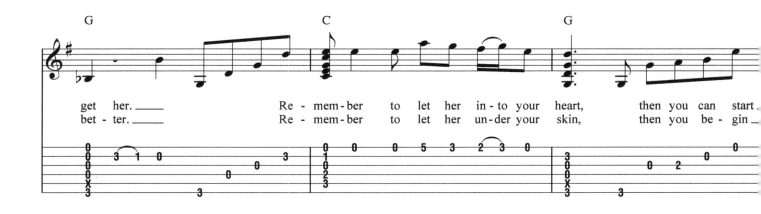

get her. _____ Re - mem - ber to let her in - to your heart, then you can start

bet - ter. _____ Re - mem - ber to let her un - der your skin, then you be - gin _____

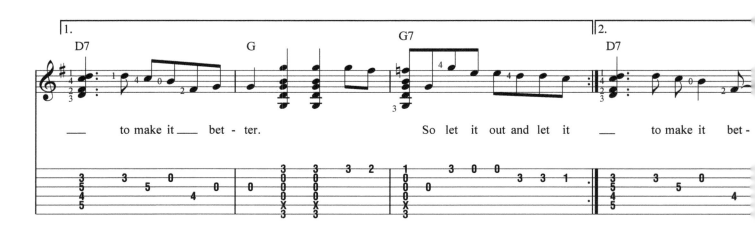

1.

_____ to make it _____ bet - ter. So let it out and let it _____ to make it bet -

2.

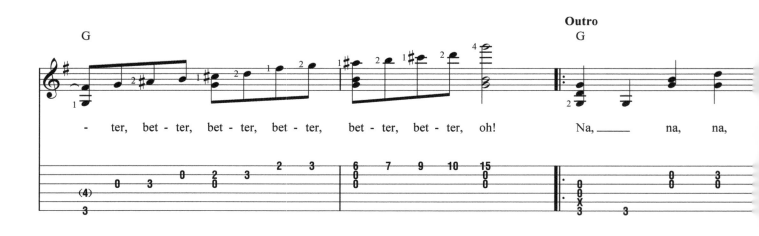

Outro

- ter, bet - ter, bet - ter, bet - ter, bet - ter, bet - ter, oh! Na, _____ na, na,

na, na, na, na, _____ na, na, na, na, _____ hey Jude.

1., 2., 3.

4.

Jude.

22

Let It Be

Words and Music by John Lennon and Paul McCartney

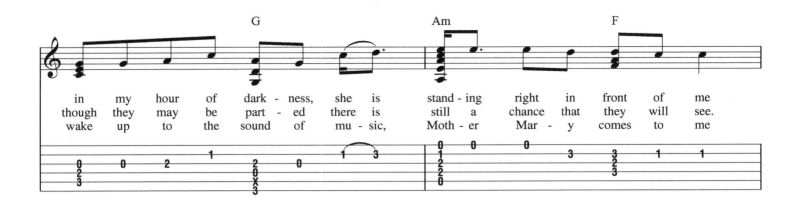

in my hour of darkness, she is standing right in front of me
though they may be parted there is still a chance that they will see.
wake up to the sound of music, Mother Mary comes to me

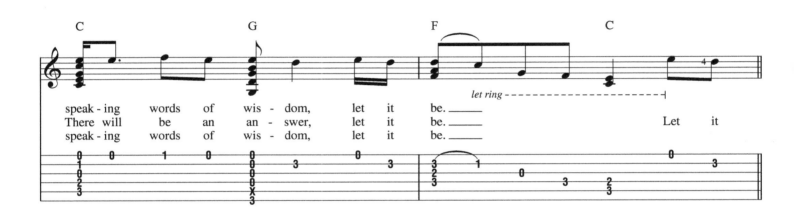

speak-ing words of wis-dom, let it be._____
There will be an an-swer, let it be._____ Let it
speak-ing words of wis-dom, let it be._____

let ring

Chorus

be, let it be. Let it be, _____ let it be.

[1.

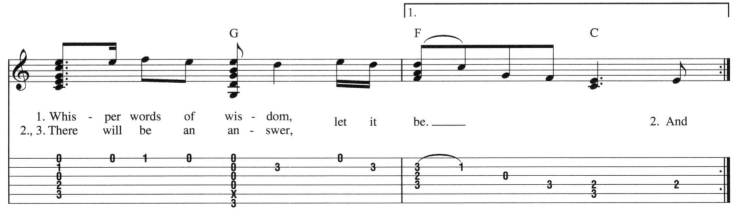

1. Whis-per words of wis-dom, let it be._____
2., 3. There will be an an-swer, 2. And

be. ____   Let it be,   let it be.   Let it be, ____

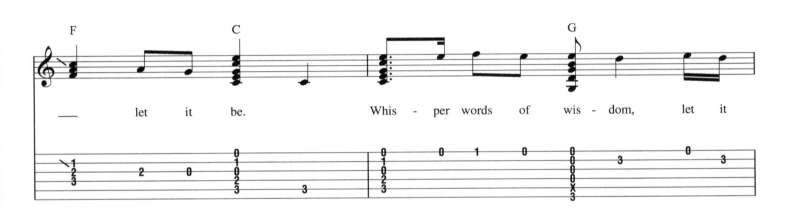

____   let it be.   Whis - per words of wis - dom, let it

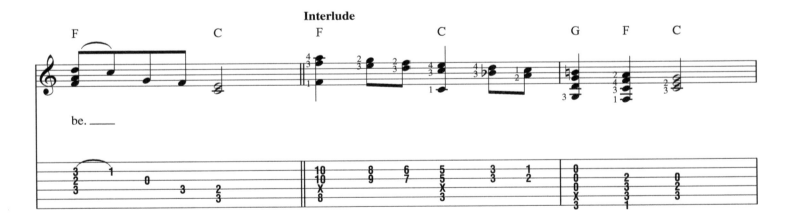

Interlude

be. ____

To Coda ⊕   *D.S. al Coda*
                   (take 2nd ending)   ⊕ **Coda**

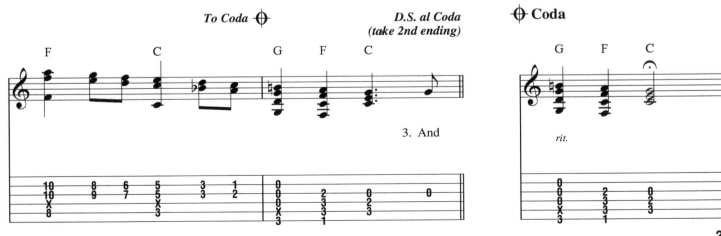

3. And

rit.

The Long and Winding Road

Words and Music by John Lennon and Paul McCartney

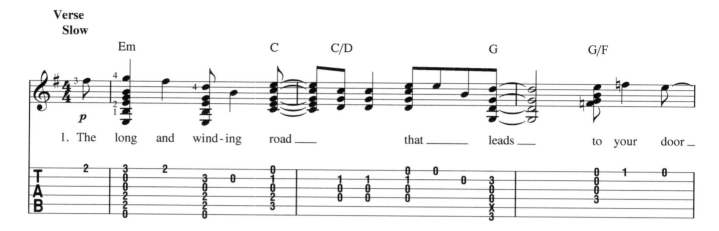

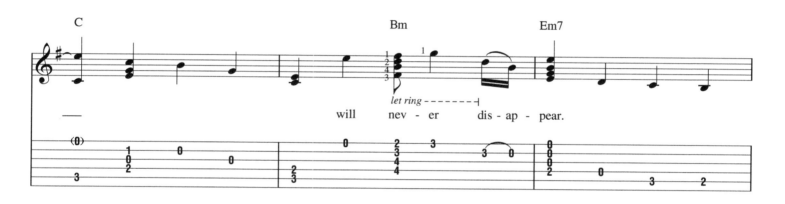

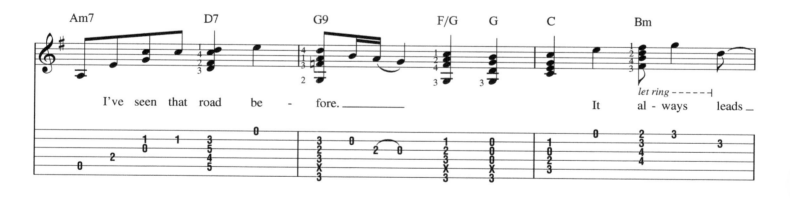

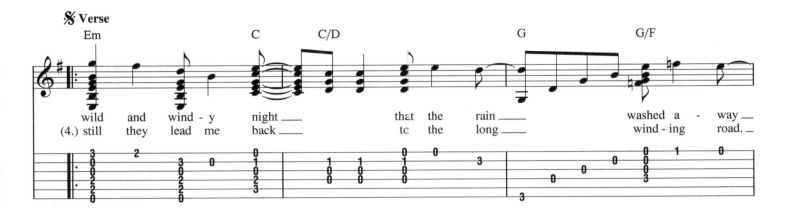

wild and wind-y night ___ that the rain ___ washed a - way ___
(4.) still they lead me back ___ to the long ___ wind - ing road. __

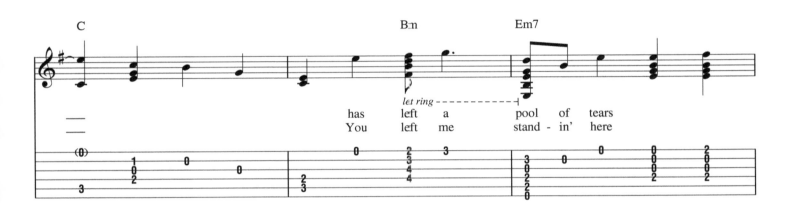

let ring - - - - - - - - - -

has left a pool of tears
You left me stand - in' here

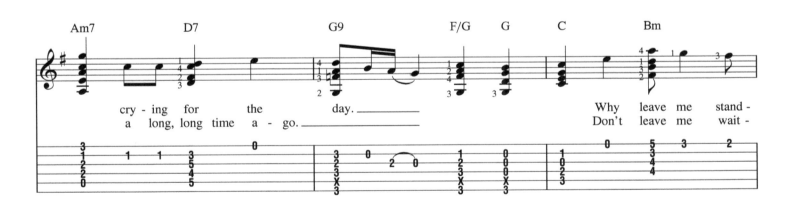

cry - ing for the day. _____ Why leave me stand -
a long, long time a - go. _____ Don't leave me wait -

To Coda ⊕

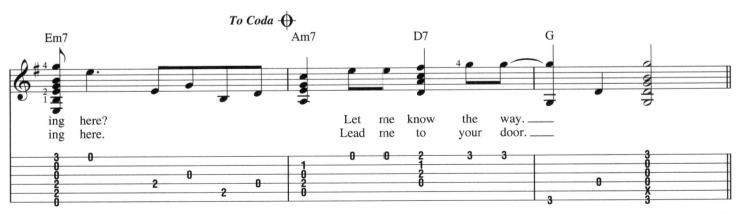

ing here? Let me know the way. ___
ing here. Lead me to your door. ___

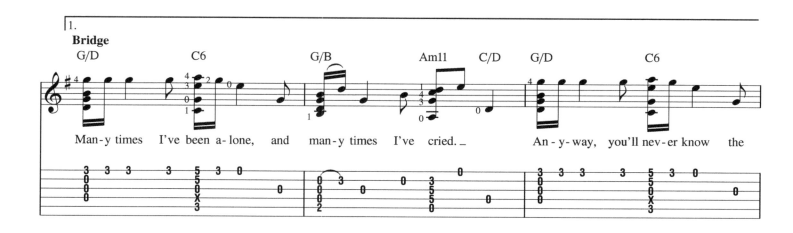

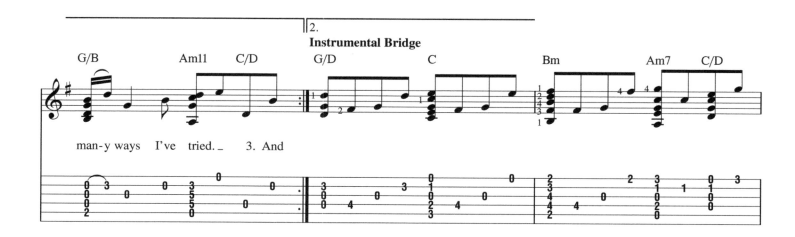

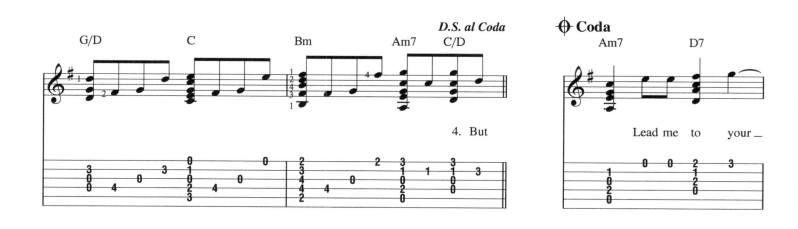

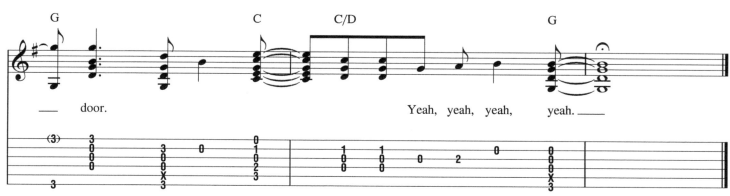

Lucy in the Sky with Diamonds

Words and Music by John Lennon and Paul McCartney

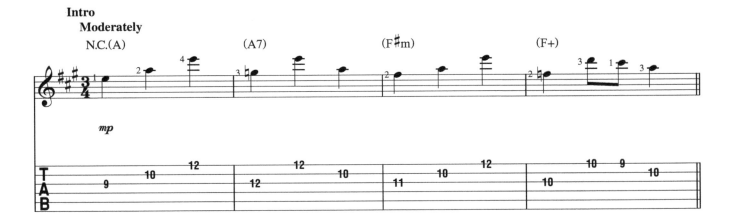

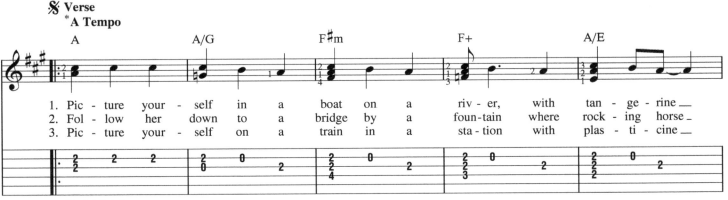

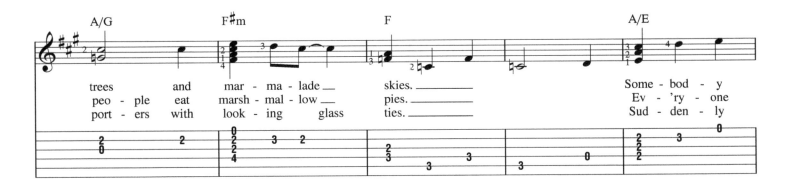

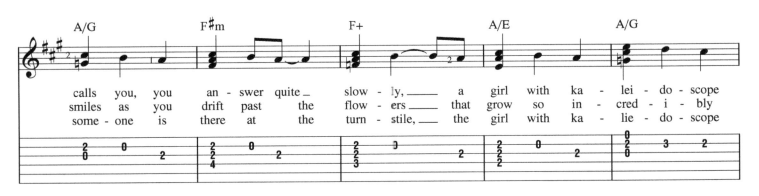

Michelle

Words and Music by John Lennon and Paul McCartney

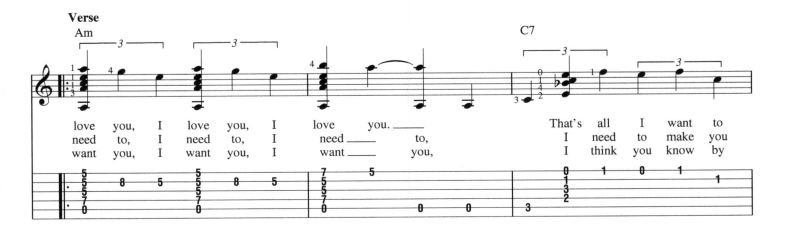

love you, I love you, I love you. ___ That's all I want to
need to, I need to, I need ___ to, I need to make you
want you, I want you, I want ___ you, I think you know by

say. Un - til I find a way, ___ I will
see, oh, what you mean to me. ___ Un -
now. I'll get to you some - how. ___ Un -

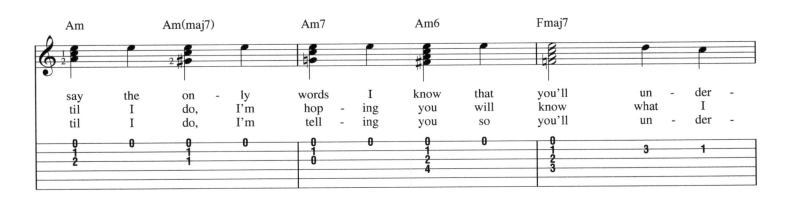

say the on - ly words I know that you'll un - der -
til I do, I'm hop - ing you will know what I
til I do, I'm tell - ing you so you'll un - der -

Chorus

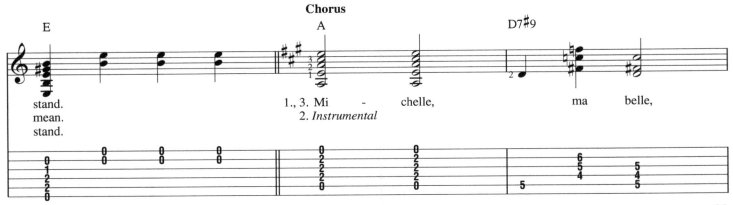

stand. 1., 3. Mi - chelle, ma belle,
mean. *2. Instrumental*
stand.

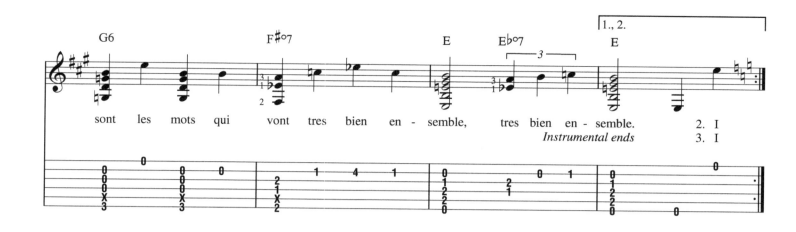

sont les mots qui vont tres bien en - semble, tres bien en - semble.

Instrumental ends

2. I
3. I

semble. And I will say the on - ly words I know that you'll un - der -

Outro-Chorus

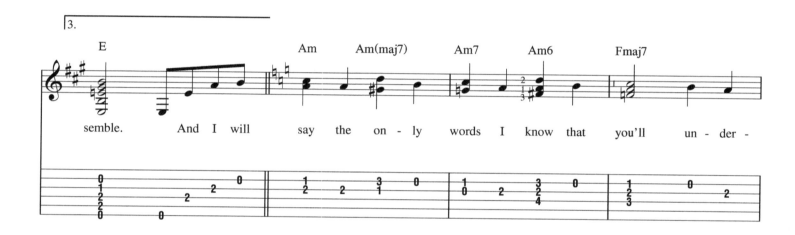

stand, my Mi - *chelle.

*Sung first time only.

You've Got to Hide Your Love Away

Words and Music by John Lennon and Paul McCartney

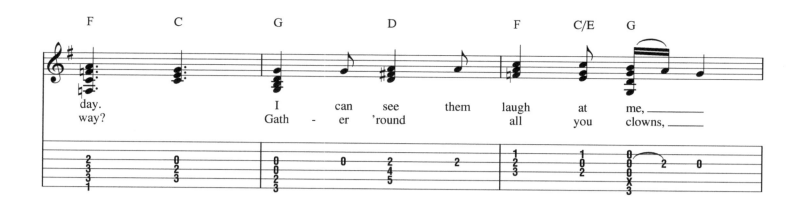

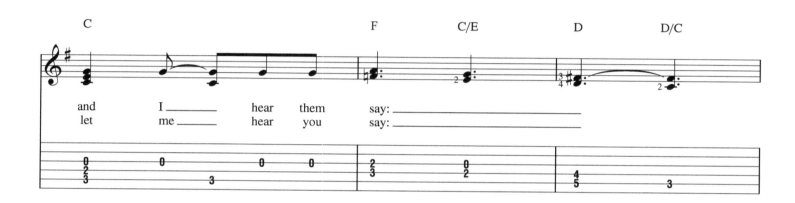

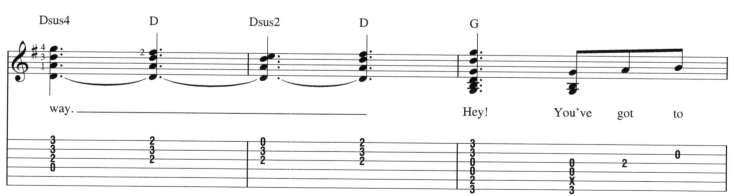

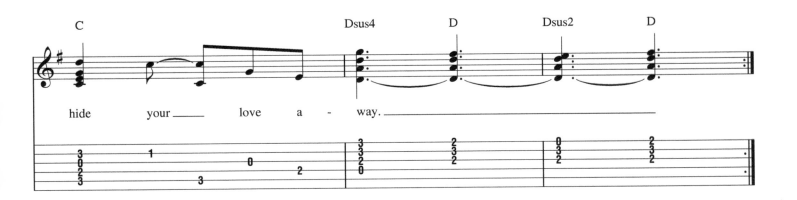

hide your love a - way.

Outro

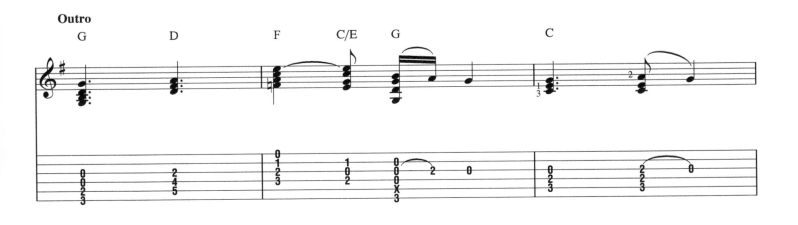

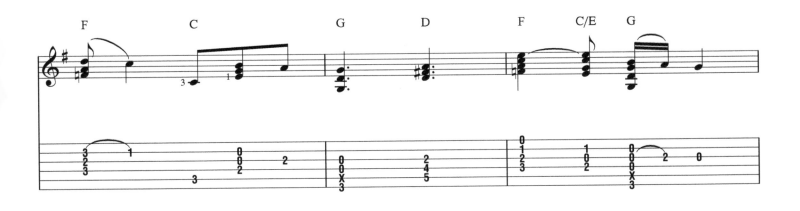

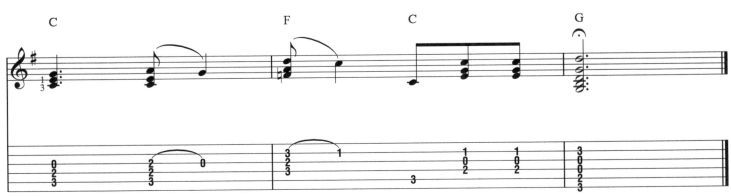

Norwegian Wood
(This Bird Has Flown)

Words and Music by John Lennon and Paul McCartney

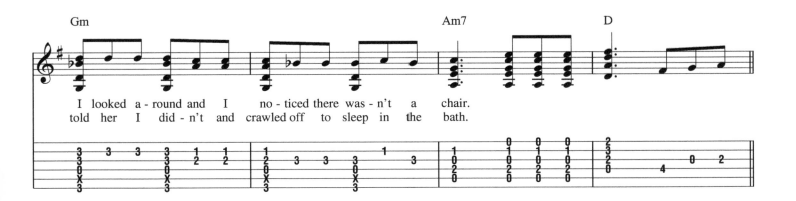

I looked a - round and I no - ticed there was - n't a chair.
told her I did - n't and crawled off to sleep in the bath.

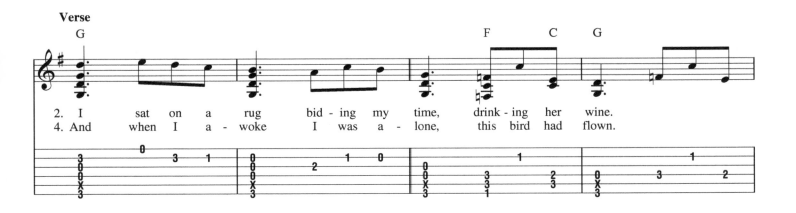

Verse

2. I sat on a rug bid - ing my time, drink - ing her wine.
4. And when I a - woke I was a - lone, this bird had flown.

We talked un - til two, and then she said, "It's time for bed."
So I lit a fire, is - n't it good, Nor - we - gian wood.

Outro

Something

Words and Music by George Harrison

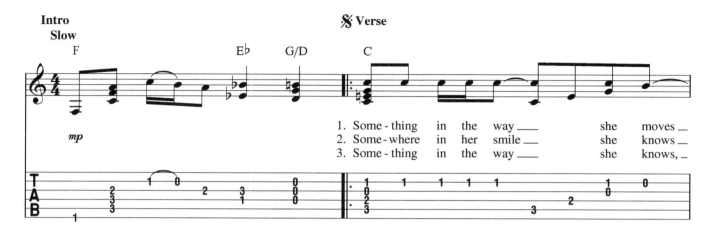

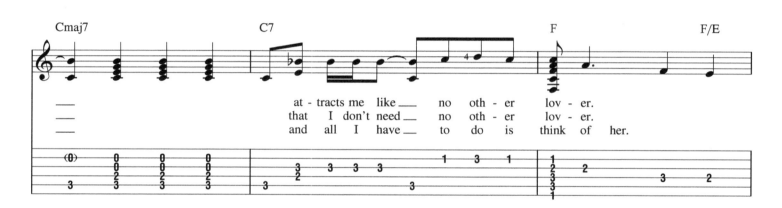

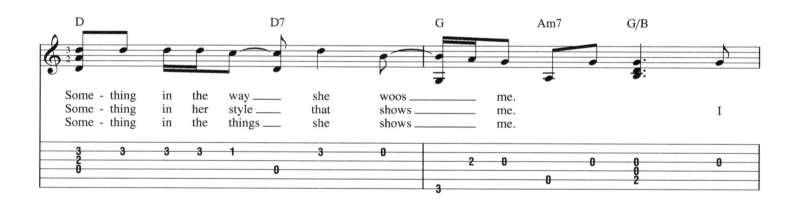

Yesterday

Words and Music by John Lennon and Paul McCartney

FINGERPICKING GUITAR BOOKS

Hone your fingerpicking skills with these great songbooks featuring solo guitar arrangements in standard notation and tablature. The arrangements in these books are carefully written for intermediate-level guitarists. Each song combines melody and harmony in one superb guitar fingerpicking arrangement. Each book also includes an introduction to basic fingerstyle guitar.

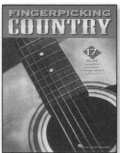

Fingerpicking Acoustic
00699614 15 songs......................$14.99

Fingerpicking Acoustic Classics
00160211 15 songs......................$16.99

Fingerpicking Acoustic Hits
00160202 15 songs......................$12.99

Fingerpicking Acoustic Rock
00699764 14 songs......................$16.99

Fingerpicking Ballads
00699717 15 songs......................$15.99

Fingerpicking Beatles
00699049 30 songs......................$24.99

Fingerpicking Beethoven
00702390 15 pieces......................$10.99

Fingerpicking Blues
00701277 15 songs $12.99

Fingerpicking Broadway Favorites
00699843 15 songs......................$9.99

Fingerpicking Broadway Hits
00699838 15 songs $7.99

Fingerpicking Campfire
00275964 15 songs......................$14.99

Fingerpicking Celtic Folk
00701148 15 songs......................$12.99

Fingerpicking Children's Songs
00699712 15 songs......................$9.99

Fingerpicking Christian
00701076 15 songs......................$12.99

Fingerpicking Christmas
00699599 20 carols......................$12.99

Fingerpicking Christmas Classics
00701695 15 songs......................$7.99

Fingerpicking Christmas Songs
00171333 15 songs......................$10.99

Fingerpicking Classical
00699620 15 pieces......................$10.99

Fingerpicking Country
00699687 17 songs......................$12.99

Fingerpicking Disney
00699711 15 songs......................$17.99

Fingerpicking Early Jazz Standards
00276565 15 songs $12.99

Fingerpicking Duke Ellington
00699845 15 songs......................$9.99

Fingerpicking Enya
00701161 15 songs......................$16.99

Fingerpicking Film Score Music
00160143 15 songs......................$12.99

Fingerpicking Gospel
00701059 15 songs......................$9.99

Fingerpicking Hit Songs
00160195 15 songs......................$12.99

Fingerpicking Hymns
00699688 15 hymns $12.99

Fingerpicking Irish Songs
00701965 15 songs......................$10.99

Fingerpicking Italian Songs
00159778 15 songs......................$12.99

Fingerpicking Jazz Favorites
00699844 15 songs......................$12.99

Fingerpicking Jazz Standards
00699840 15 songs......................$12.99

Fingerpicking Elton John
00237495 15 songs......................$15.99

Fingerpicking Latin Favorites
00699842 15 songs......................$12.99

Fingerpicking Latin Standards
00699837 15 songs......................$17.99

Fingerpicking Andrew Lloyd Webber
00699839 14 songs......................$16.99

Fingerpicking Love Songs
00699841 15 songs......................$14.99

Fingerpicking Love Standards
00699836 15 songs $9.99

Fingerpicking Lullabyes
00701276 16 songs......................$9.99

Fingerpicking Movie Music
00699919 15 songs......................$14.99

Fingerpicking Mozart
00699794 15 pieces......................$10.99

Fingerpicking Pop
00699615 15 songs......................$14.99

Fingerpicking Popular Hits
00139079 14 songs......................$12.99

Fingerpicking Praise
00699714 15 songs......................$14.99

Fingerpicking Rock
00699716 15 songs......................$14.99

Fingerpicking Standards
00699613 17 songs......................$15.99

Fingerpicking Wedding
00699637 15 songs......................$10.99

Fingerpicking Worship
00700554 15 songs......................$14.99

Fingerpicking Neil Young – Greatest Hits
00700134 16 songs......................$17.99

Fingerpicking Yuletide
00699654 16 songs......................$12.99

HAL•LEONARD®

Order these and more great publications from your favorite music retailer at
halleonard.com

Prices, contents and availability subject to change without notice.

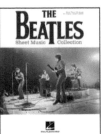

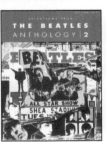

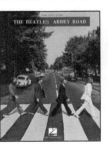

The Beatles Complete
Volume 1
103 songs from A-I: All You Need Is Love • Back in the U.S.S.R. • Blackbird • Come Together • Day Tripper • Eleanor Rigby • The Fool on the Hill • Hello, Goodbye • I Want to Hold Your Hand • and more.
00356240 Piano/Vocal/Guitar $32.50

Volume 2
104 songs from I-Y: In My Life • Let It Be • Lucy in the Sky with Diamonds • Norwegian Wood • Paperback Writer • Twist and Shout • When I'm Sixty Four • With a Little Help from My Friends • Yesterday • and more.
00356241 Piano/Vocal/Guitar $32.50

The Beatles – 1
27 British and American Number One singles: Can't Buy Me Love • Eight Days a Week • Get Back • A Hard Day's Night • Hey Jude • Love Me Do • Ticket to Ride • We Can Work It Out • Yellow Submarine • Yesterday • and more.
00306411 Piano/Vocal/Guitar $22.99

Selections from The Beatles Anthology
Volume 1
Free As a Bird and 26 more classics: From Me to You • A Hard Day's Night • Hello Little Girl • Love Me Do • Money • Please Please Me • She Loves You • Twist and Shout • You Really Got a Hold on Me • and more.
00306076 Piano/Vocal/Guitar $19.99

Volume 2
Hello, Goodbye • Help! • I Am the Walrus • Lady Madonna • Lucy in the Sky with Diamonds • Norwegian Wood • Penny Lane • Real Love • Strawberry Fields Forever • Ticket to Ride • and more.
00306103 Piano/Vocal/Guitar $17.95

Volume 3
All Things Must Pass • Blackbird • Cry Baby Cry • The End • Hey Jude • I'm So Tired • Junk • Let It Be • Piggies • Why Don't We Do It in the Road • and more.
00306144 Piano/Vocal/Guitar $17.95

The Beatles – The Capitol Albums
Volume 1
Volume 1 features 42 songs from The Beatles' original Capitol recordings: All My Loving • And I Love Her • I Saw Her Standing There • I Want to Hold Your Hand • If I Fell • She Loves You • You Can't Do That • and dozens more.
00306840 Piano/Vocal/Guitar $19.95

Volume 2
45 more songs from the Capitol collections, including: Hard Day's Night • Do You Want to Know a Secret? • Eight Days a Week • Help! • I've Just Seen a Face • Michelle • Norwegian Wood • Please Please Me • Ticket to Ride • Twist and Shout • and more.
00306841 Piano/Vocal/Guitar $19.95

The Beatles – 1962-1966
26 of their greatest early hits: And I Love Her • Day Tripper • Eight Days a Week • I Want to Hold Your Hand • Love Me Do • Yellow Submarine • Yesterday • more.
00306373 Piano/Vocal/Guitar $19.95

The Beatles – 1967-1970
28 more classics: All You Need Is Love • The Ballad of John and Yoko • Hey Jude • Penny Lane • Revolution • Strawberry Fields Forever • and more.
00306374 Piano/Vocal/Guitar $22.99

Beatles Ballads – 2nd Edition
32 songs, including: And I Love Her • Blackbird • Here, There and Everywhere • Let It Be • Norwegian Wood (This Bird Has Flown) • Yesterday • and more.
00308236 Piano/Vocal/Guitar $16.99

Beatles Best – 2nd Edition
More than 120 Beatles hits: All My Loving • And I Love Her • Come Together • Eleanor Rigby • Get Back • Help! • Hey Jude • I Want to Hold Your Hand • Let It Be • Michelle • many, many more.
00356223 Piano/Vocal/Guitar $34.99

The Beatles – Live at the Hollywood Bowl
16 songs from the 2016 album release: All My Loving • Baby's in Black • Boys • Can't Buy Me Love • Dizzy Miss Lizzie • Everybody's Trying to Be My Baby • A Hard Day's Night • Help! • I Want to Hold Your Hand • Long Tall Sally • She Loves You • She's a Woman • Things We Said Today • Ticket to Ride • Twist and Shout • You Can't Do That.
00202247 Piano/Vocal/Guitar $16.99

Love Songs of the Beatles – 2nd Edition
This second edition has been revised to include 25 favorite love songs from the Fab Four, including: All My Loving • All You Need Is Love • And I Love Her • Eight Days a Week • From Me to You • Girl • Here, There and Everywhere • Hey Jude • I Want to Hold Your Hand • In My Life • Love Me Do • Michelle • Something • Yesterday • and more.
00356224 Piano/Vocal/Guitar $14.99

The Beatles Sheet Music Collection
440 pages featuring over 100 timeless hits, including: All My Loving • Blackbird • Can't Buy Me Love • Don't Let Me Down • Eight Days a Week • Eleanor Rigby • Here Comes the Sun • Hey Jude • I Want to Hold Your Hand • In My Life • Let It Be • Norwegian Wood (This Bird Has Flown) • Ob-La-Di, Ob-La-Da • Penny Lane • Revolution • Twist and Shout • When I'm Sixty-Four • Yesterday • and more.
00236171 Piano/Vocal/Guitar $34.99

The Beatles – Abbey Road
All 17 songs from the classic album: Carry That Weight • Come Together • Golden Slumbers • Here Comes the Sun • Maxwell's Silver Hammer • Something • and more.
00295914 Piano/Vocal/Guitar $16.99

The Beatles – Revolver
All 14 tracks from the 1966 Beatles album that includes classic hits like: Eleanor Rigby • Good Day Sunshine • Got to Get You into My Life • Here, There and Everywhere • I Want to Tell You • Taxman • Yellow Submarine • and more!
00295911 Piano/Vocal/Guitar $16.99

The Beatles – Sgt. Pepper's Lonely Hearts Club Band
Matching folio to classic album. 12 songs, including: With a Little Help from My Friends • Lucy in the Sky with Diamonds • When I'm Sixty Four • A Day in the Life.
00358168 Piano/Vocal/Guitar $16.99

The Beatles – Yellow Submarine/The White Album
30 songs from these albums: All You Need Is Love • Back in the USSR • Birthday • Blackbird • Ob-La-Di, Ob-La-Da • Revolution • While My Guitar Gently Weeps • Yellow Submarine • many more.
00356236 Piano/Vocal/Guitar $19.95

The Beatles – Yellow Submarine
15 classic songs, including: All Together Now • Eleanor Rigby • Lucy in the Sky with Diamonds • Sgt. Pepper's Lonely Hearts Club Band • When I'm Sixty-Four • With a Little Help from My Friends • Yellow Submarine • & more.
00313146 Piano/Vocal/Guitar $16.99

Beatlemania
1967-1970 (Volume 2)
45 of the Beatles biggest hits from 1967-1970, including: All You Need Is Love • Come Together • Hey Jude • Let It Be • The Long and Winding Road • Penny Lane • Revolution • many more!
00356222 Piano/Vocal/Guitar $19.95

JAZZ GUITAR CHORD MELODY SOLOS

This series features chord melody arrangements in standard notation and tablature of songs for intermediate guitarists. **INCLUDES TAB**

ALL-TIME STANDARDS
27 songs, including: All of Me • Bewitched • Come Fly with Me • A Fine Romance • Georgia on My Mind • How High the Moon • I'll Never Smile Again • I've Got You Under My Skin • It's De-Lovely • It's Only a Paper Moon • My Romance • Satin Doll • The Surrey with the Fringe on Top • Yesterdays • and more.
00699757 Solo Guitar...........................$16.99

IRVING BERLIN
27 songs, including: Alexander's Ragtime Band • Always • Blue Skies • Cheek to Cheek • Easter Parade • Happy Holiday • Heat Wave • How Deep Is the Ocean • Puttin' On the Ritz • Remember • They Say It's Wonderful • What'll I Do? • White Christmas • and more.
00700637 Solo Guitar...........................$14.99

CHRISTMAS CAROLS
26 songs, including: Auld Lang Syne • Away in a Manger • Deck the Hall • God Rest Ye Merry, Gentlemen • Good King Wenceslas • Here We Come A-Wassailing • It Came upon the Midnight Clear • Joy to the World • O Holy Night • O Little Town of Bethlehem • Silent Night • Toyland • We Three Kings of Orient Are • and more.
00701697 Solo Guitar $14.99

CHRISTMAS JAZZ
21 songs, including Auld Lang Syne • Baby, It's Cold Outside • Cool Yule • Have Yourself a Merry Little Christmas • I've Got My Love to Keep Me Warm • Mary, Did You Know? • Santa Baby • Sleigh Ride • White Christmas • Winter Wonderland • and more.
00171334 Solo Guitar $15.99

DISNEY SONGS
27 songs, including: Beauty and the Beast • Can You Feel the Love Tonight • Candle on the Water • Colors of the Wind • A Dream Is a Wish Your Heart Makes • Heigh-Ho • Some Day My Prince Will Come • Under the Sea • When You Wish upon a Star • A Whole New World (Aladdin's Theme) • Zip-A-Dee-Doo-Dah • and more.
00701902 Solo Guitar $14.99

DUKE ELLINGTON
25 songs, including: C-Jam Blues • Caravan • Do Nothin' Till You Hear from Me • Don't Get Around Much Anymore • I Got It Bad and That Ain't Good • I'm Just a Lucky So and So • In a Sentimental Mood • It Don't Mean a Thing (If It Ain't Got That Swing) • Mood Indigo • Perdido • Prelude to a Kiss • Satin Doll • and more.
00700636 Solo Guitar $14.99

FAVORITE STANDARDS
27 songs, including: All the Way • Autumn in New York • Blue Skies • Cheek to Cheek • Don't Get Around Much Anymore • How Deep Is the Ocean • I'll Be Seeing You • Isn't It Romantic? • It Could Happen to You • The Lady Is a Tramp • Moon River • Speak Low • Take the "A" Train • Willow Weep for Me • Witchcraft • and more.
00699756 Solo Guitar $17.99

JAZZ BALLADS
27 songs, including: Body and Soul • Darn That Dream • Easy to Love (You'd Be So Easy to Love) • Here's That Rainy Day • In a Sentimental Mood • Misty • My Foolish Heart • My Funny Valentine • The Nearness of You • Stella by Starlight • Time After Time • The Way You Look Tonight • When Sunny Gets Blue • and more.
00699755 Solo Guitar...........................$16.99

LATIN STANDARDS
27 Latin favorites, including: Água De Beber (Water to Drink) • Desafinado • The Girl from Ipanema • How Insensitive (Insensatez) • Little Boat • Meditation • One Note Samba (Samba De Uma Nota So) • Poinciana • Quiet Nights of Quiet Stars • Samba De Orfeu • So Nice (Summer Samba) • Wave • and more.
00699754 Solo Guitar...........................$16.99

Order online at **halleonard.com**

HAL•LEONARD®